OCT   2010

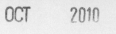

Mixtures
and Solutions

Carol Ballard

www.heinemannraintree.com
Visit our website to find out
more information about
Heinemann-Raintree books.

To order:
☎ Phone 888-454-2279
▭ Visit www.heinemannraintree.com
  to browse our catalog and order online.

Edited by Annabel Savery
Designed by Rob Walster, Big Blu Design.
Original illustrations © Discovery Books Limited 2009
Illustrated by Stefan Chabluk
Picture research by Annabel Savery and Rachel Tisdale
Originated by Modern Age
Printed and bound in China by South China Printing
  Company Ltd

13 12 11 10 09
10 9 8 7 6 5 4 3 2 1

Library of Congress Cataloging-in-Publication Data
Ballard, Carol.
  Mixtures and solutions / Carol Ballard.
    p. cm. -- (Sci-hi. Physical science)
  Includes bibliographical references and index.
  ISBN 978-1-4109-3376-8 (hc)
  -- ISBN 978-1-4109-3381-2 (pb)
  1. Solution (Chemistry)--Juvenile literature.
  2. Mixtures--Juvenile literature.
  3. Molecules--Juvenile literature.
  4. Chemistry--Juvenile literature.
  I. Title.
  QD541.B33 2010
  541'.34--dc22
                              2009013452

Acknowledgments
We would like to thank the following for permission to
reproduce photographs: Getty Images: pp. **25** (Dorling
Kindersley), **39** (Jeff Gross); Science Photo Library: pp.
35 main (Andrew Lambert Photography), **36** (Peggy
Greb/US Department of Agriculture), **38** (Patrick
Landmann); Shutterstock: pp. **3** top, **4**, **5**, **6** (Gayane), **7**,
8, **9**, **11** top & bottom, **13** (Simone Van den Berg), **14**,
16, **17**, **19**, **20**, **21**, **22** (Simone Van den Berg), **24**, **26**,
27, **31**, **34** & **35** bottom, **35**, **37**.

Cover photograph of test tubes and beaker
reproduced with permission
of Alamy Images.

We would like to thank content consultant Suzy
Gazlay and text consultant Nancy Harris for their
invaluable help in the preparation of this book.

Every effort has been made to contact copyright
holders of material reproduced in this book. Any
omissions will be rectified in subsequent printings if
notice is given to the publishers.

Contents

If a seabird is covered with oil, what is the best solvent to use to clean it? Find out on page 17!

How is salt collected from saltwater? Find out on page 27!

Some words are shown in bold, **like this**. These words are explained in the glossary. You will find important information and definitions underlined, **<u>like this</u>**.

What is a Mixture?

What links paint, smoke, and whipped cream? They are very different from each other, but they all have one thing in common: they are mixtures. This means that they each contain two or more things mixed together.

The granola in this bowl is a mixture of lots of different things.

Granola mixture

Think of a bowl of granola. It contains all sorts of things, such as wheat flakes, nuts, rice, pieces of fruit, oats, and bran. If you had time, you could sort each thing into separate bowls. The granola is a mixture. It is made of two or more different things mixed together, but each can be separated from the rest. They are not joined together in any way. But to understand mixtures, you have to know a bit about the things they are made from—so read on . . .

Particles everywhere!

Just as the granola is made up of lots of small bits, everything around you is made up of small bits, too. These are called **particles**, and they are very, very small. They are so small that millions would fit on the point of a pin!

The smallest particles of a substance are called **atoms**. Atoms can join together to make larger particles called **molecules**.

Mixtures

Mixtures are made from more than one type of molecule. The molecules are not joined together, so they can easily be separated.

Here are some common mixtures that you might find every day:

☆ Saltwater is a mixture of salt molecules and water molecules.

☆ Air is a mixture of lots of different **gases**.

☆ Ink is a mixture of water and different colored dyes.

☆ Paint is a mixture of colored **pigments** and many other substances.

Types of mixtures

Mixtures are made by putting molecules of different substances together. There are two types of mixtures:

Homogeneous mixtures

Homogeneous mixtures are the same throughout. An example is seawater. Salt is spread evenly through the water and one part is not saltier than another. The mixture has the **properties**, or features, of each of the substances that it contains. Saltwater is a clear **liquid**, like water, but it also has the taste of salt.

Soapy water, wine, shampoo, and ink are all homogeneous mixtures.

Liquid soap, which you can use to blow bubbles, is a homogeneous mixture.

WHAT ARE PROPERTIES?

A property of a substance is a characteristic that it has. For example, the **metal** aluminum is very light, so lightness is a property of aluminum. Other common properties of substances include being shiny or dull, hard or soft, rough or smooth.

Sand is a heterogeneous mixture of tiny pieces of stone, shell, and other materials.

Heterogeneous mixtures

Heterogeneous mixtures are not the same throughout. For example, a salad is a mixture of vegetables. One forkful might have a lot of tomatoes and another might have a lot of lettuce. Each of the substances that make the mixture keeps its own properties. The lettuce and tomato each keep their own different looks and tastes when you mix them up in a salad.

Granola, soil, noodle soup, fruit salad, and sand on a beach are all heterogeneous mixtures.

Try This!

Making mixtures

Sometimes, you can turn a heterogeneous mixture into a homogeneous mixture! Try this:

Add some chocolate milk powder to water. You will be able to see the clear water and the grains of the powder. You have made a heterogeneous mixture.

Now stir the mixture. The grains will be evenly distributed throughout the water. You can no longer tell one from the other. You have turned it into a homogeneous mixture!

Elements and compounds

The mixture saltwater contains salt and water. Each of these substances is a **compound** whose molecules are made up from atoms of **elements**.

Elements

Elements are pure substances. Each element is made up of a single type of atom. The atoms of one element are different from the atoms of other elements. The atoms and the way they are arranged together give each element its own special properties.

Gold, silver, iron, carbon, oxygen, and calcium are all elements.

Elements can be mixed together to make mixtures. For example, "white gold" jewelry is made by mixing gold with another metal, such as palladium.

These diamonds are made from atoms of the element carbon.

Graphite and diamond

Some atoms can be arranged in more than one way to give two different forms of an element. Graphite, which is used for pencil "lead," is a soft black **solid**. It is made of carbon atoms arranged in layers of hexagons, sort of like a honeycomb. Diamond, which is hard and shiny, is also made of carbon atoms, but the atoms are arranged to form a network of cubes.

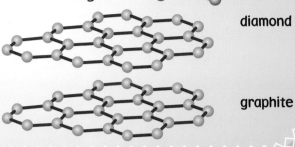

diamond

graphite

Compounds

The elements in a mixture might go through a **chemical reaction**. This is a change that creates a new substance. The new substance is called a compound.

During a chemical reaction, the atoms in different elements join together to make molecules. These molecules form the new compound. To separate the elements again, another chemical reaction would be needed. This would break the molecules apart again into separate atoms.

A compound has different properties from the substances from which it is made. For example, the white crystals that we use as table salt are a compound. Salt is made from a silvery metal called sodium and a very smelly gas called chlorine!

Rust, salt, plastic, sugar, chalk, and bronze are all compounds.

Rust is a compound made from iron and oxygen. A chemical reaction is needed to make the shiny metal turn into brown rust.

Solid, liquid, or gas?

Elements, mixtures, and compounds can exist as solids, liquids, or gases. These are called the **states of matter**. The particles of a substance are always the same, whether it is a solid, liquid, or gas. All that changes is the way they are arranged. Look at how this works:

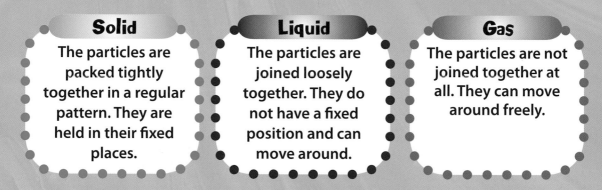

Solid
The particles are packed tightly together in a regular pattern. They are held in their fixed places.

Liquid
The particles are joined loosely together. They do not have a fixed position and can move around.

Gas
The particles are not joined together at all. They can move around freely.

Heating and cooling

You can change a substance from a **solid** to a **liquid**, and then to a **gas** by heating it. If you cool it, the opposite happens. The arrangement of the particles that make up the substance changes as the temperature changes.

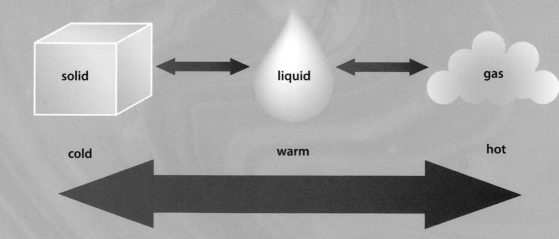

solid   liquid   gas

cold   warm   hot

Water

Water is a compound. It is made from the elements hydrogen and oxygen. Water is the only natural substance that is found in all three states of matter—solid, liquid, and gas—at temperatures normally found on Earth. It can exist as:

solid ice, as in icebergs and icicles,

liquid water, as in rivers and rain,

gas, as in steam from thermal springs.

A mixture of gases

The air all around you is a mixture. It contains different gases. Some gases, such as nitrogen and oxygen, are elements. Other gases, such as carbon dioxide and water vapor, are compounds.

Air is 78.08 percent nitrogen, 20.95 percent oxygen, 0.93 percent argon, 0.03 percent carbon dioxide, and traces of other gases.

Plasmas

We usually think about three states of matter: solid, liquid, and gas. But there is a fourth state, too, called **plasma**. Amazingly, this is actually the most common form of matter in the universe! Plasma is created when atoms in a gas break down. Plasma glows when an electric current (a flow of electricity) is passed through it.

Plasmas are used in neon lights. Different gases give different colors.

What Is a Solution?

A solution is a homogeneous mixture. Molecules of one substance are spread evenly throughout another substance. The molecules of each substance do not join together, though. This means the mixture can be separated into the two original substances. Sugar mixed in water is a solution. Many solutions are liquids, but some are not.

Important words

word	what it means	example
solute	the substance that is going to **dissolve**	sugar
solvent	the substance in which the solute will dissolve	water
solution	the solute and solvent mixed together	result of mixing sugar in water
dissolve	to mix a solute into a solvent to form a solution	sugar dissolves in the water to make a sugar solution
soluble	the solute can dissolve in the solvent	sugar—it can dissolve in water
insoluble	the solute cannot dissolve in the solvent	chalk—it cannot dissolve in water

+

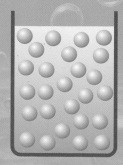

solute

=

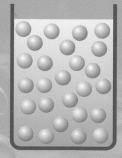

solvent

solution

Sweat is a solution of chemicals (substances with certain **properties**) dissolved in water. These chemicals can include ammonia, salts, and sugar.

More than one solute

Many solutions are made up of one solute dissolved in one solvent. But many solutions contain two or more solutes! Sweat and tears are like this—they each contain several different **chemicals**.

What happens when a solid dissolves in a liquid?

If you stir sugar into water, the sugar **dissolves**. You cannot see it any more, but the water tastes sweet and sugary. So where has the sugar gone?

Into the gaps

The **particles** in a liquid are spread out evenly. They are joined loosely together and can move about freely within the liquid. There are lots of spaces in between them. When a **solid** is added, the particles of solid move into the spaces between the **liquid** particles.

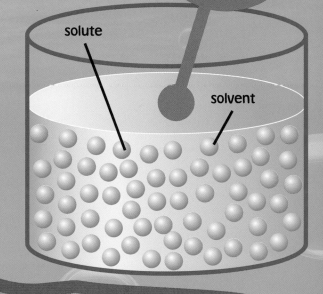

Solute particles spread out evenly in the spaces between the solvent particles.

solute

solvent

Acid rain

Acid rain forms as a result of air pollution. **Compounds**, such as sulfur dioxide and nitrogen oxides, are released into the air by factories and traffic. These compounds dissolve in the water droplets in the air. The water droplets fall to Earth as rain. Clean rain is not acidic. But rain with these dissolved compounds in it is acidic. It damages the surfaces of stones, such as limestone, eating it away. Acid rain also harms plants and wildlife.

Try This!

Measuring mass

Try this to find out more about solutions:

Draw a table like this:

what you measure	mass (in g)
sugar	
jar	
jar + water	
jar + sugar solution	
water	
A	
B	

You will need:
- glass or small jar
- spoon
- spoonful of sugar
- water
- small scale, such as a food scale

1　Measure the mass of a large spoonful of sugar.

2　Measure the mass of an empty jar.

3　Half-fill the jar with water and measure the mass of the jar and water together.

4　Mix the sugar into the water. Measure the mass of the jar and sugar solution.

Now you can do some math:

Find the mass of the water by subtracting jar from jar + water. Write it down.

Add the mass of the water to the mass of the sugar. Write it down. This is answer A.

Now find out the mass of the sugar solution. Take the mass of the jar away from the mass of the jar + sugar solution. This is answer B.

Compare answer A and B. Are they the same? They should be! You don't gain or lose anything when you make a solution, so the mass of the solution has to be the same as the total mass of everything that is in it.

Different solvents

More substances will dissolve in water than in any other solvent! That is why water is often known as the "universal solvent." However, some substances do not dissolve in water. To make them dissolve, you have to use a different solvent.

Using other solvents

Sometimes other solvents are very useful! Here are some examples:

Nail varnish does not come off when you wash your hands. It is not soluble in water. If you want to remove it, you have to use a different solvent. Nail varnish removers are liquids that contain the solvents acetone or ethyl acetate.

Some fabrics are damaged if they are washed in water. So, instead, people take them to be "dry cleaned." Dry cleaning is not really dry, it just doesn't use water. Instead, it uses a different solvent, usually a chemical called tetrachloroethylene.

Some paints are not soluble in water, so you can't use water to clean your paintbrushes. Instead, solvents such as turpentine and toluene are used, because paint does dissolve in these. When you dip your paintbrushes in turpentine, the paint dissolves in the liquid and comes off the brush.

Nail varnish does not dissolve in water, so a different solvent is used to remove it.

Choosing the right solvent

How do you choose the right solvent for a particular job? Look at the example below. If a seabird is covered with oil from a tanker spillage, what could you use to clean it? You must use a solvent that will dissolve oil and is safe to use on birds.

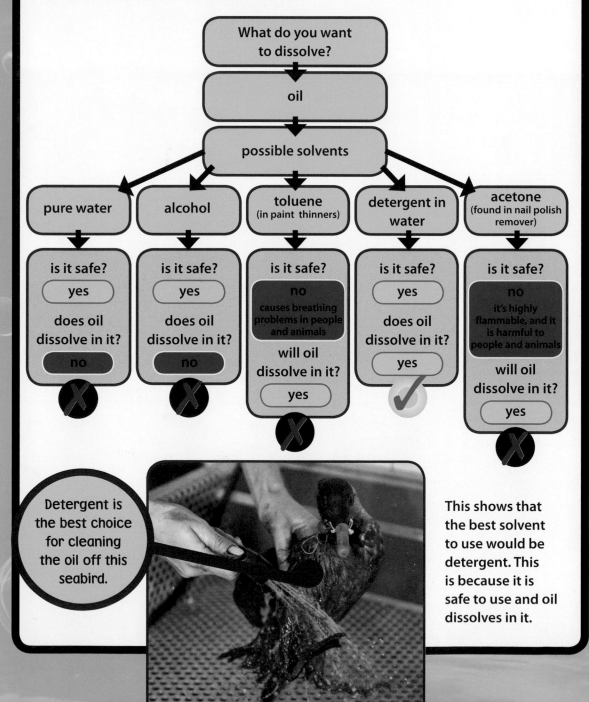

What do you want to dissolve?

oil

possible solvents

| pure water | alcohol | toluene (in paint thinners) | detergent in water | acetone (found in nail polish remover) |

pure water
is it safe?
yes
does oil dissolve in it?
no
✗

alcohol
is it safe?
yes
does oil dissolve in it?
no
✗

toluene
is it safe?
no
causes breathing problems in people and animals
will oil dissolve in it?
yes
✗

detergent in water
is it safe?
yes
does oil dissolve in it?
yes
✓

acetone
is it safe?
no
it's highly flammable, and it is harmful to people and animals
will oil dissolve in it?
yes
✗

Detergent is the best choice for cleaning the oil off this seabird.

This shows that the best solvent to use would be detergent. This is because it is safe to use and oil dissolves in it.

Suspensions and aerosols

Some substances do not dissolve in a particular solvent. They are **insoluble**. Some can be mixed with a solvent, though, to make a **suspension** or an **aerosol**.

Suspensions

A suspension is a liquid containing solid particles evenly spread through it. The solute particles in the suspension do not dissolve in the solvent. This means that they will eventually settle out.

If you mix flour and water, you make a suspension. The flour particles are spread through the water at first. Slowly, though, they will sink to the bottom of the container.

Aerosols

An aerosol is a suspension of liquid droplets or fine solid particles in a **gas**. Some occur naturally. For example, when a volcano erupts, particles of dust and ash are released into the air. The particles slowly settle out onto the ground. Other aerosols are **human-made**. For example, asthma inhalers contain an aerosol of gas and medicine.

Using an inhaler delivers an aerosol of gas and medicine directly into the lungs.

These oil droplets won't mix with water, no matter how hard you try!

Won't mix !

Some things just cannot be mixed together! An example is oil and water. You can see this if you add a few drops of cooking oil to a jar of water—the oil just sits on top of the water. Even if you stir them up, the oil will still separate out.

This is because **oil molecules** are more attracted to each other than to water molecules. Also, water molecules are more attracted to each other than to oil molecules. So no matter how hard you try to mix them, the two types of molecules always separate themselves out again. Substances like this that cannot be mixed together are called **immiscible**.

COLLOIDS AND ALLOYS

Did you know that when you eat cheese you are eating a special mixture called a colloid? Or that a penny is made from a mixture called an alloy?

Colloids

Colloids are **homogeneous** mixtures that look like **solutions**. They are not normal solutions because the **particles** do not **dissolve**. However, they don't settle out like the particles in a **suspension**. So colloids are in between solutions and suspensions.

Colloids are formed when the particles are small enough to spread out evenly, but too big to dissolve.

Colloids can contain particles of **solid**, **liquid**, or **gas**. These can be spread out in a solid, liquid, or gas. The only combination that doesn't form a colloid is gas particles in a gas.

Hard cheeses like these are colloids. They are made from particles of liquid spread out in a solid.

This table shows some common colloids. For example, smoke is made up of solid particles spread out in a gas.

Spread out in	Particles		
	solid	**liquid**	**gas**
solid	colored glass	cheese, jelly	polystyrene foam
liquid	some colored inks	milk, mayonnaise	whipped cream
gas	smoke	fog, cloud	none

Alloys

Pick up a silver-colored coin. It's not pure silver at all! It's made from an alloy! Alloys are solid solutions. They are made by melting and mixing a **metal** and one or more additional **elements**. Alloys have metallic **properties** even though they may contain a nonmetal, such as carbon. An alloy may have some similar properties to those of its components, but it is always harder than either of the individual elements from which it is made.

Steel is an alloy of iron and carbon. It is a good material to use in building because it is very strong.

Below are some common alloys

Alloy	Made from	Properties	Used for
steel	iron and carbon	very strong	buildings, industry
brass	copper and zinc	smooth, looks like gold	locks, musical instruments
bronze	copper and tin or zinc	strong, heavy	statues, church bells
sterling silver	silver and copper	harder than pure silver	ornaments, jewelry

SOLUBILITY

Some substances are more soluble than others. For example, ammonium nitrate and potassium nitrate are two substances used in explosives and fertilizers. They are very different in terms of solubility.

Ammonium nitrate is more than three times as soluble as potassium nitrate. This means that if each of these substances is **dissolved** in the same amount of water, more than three times as much ammonium nitrate will dissolve before it starts settling out. Solubility is a measure of how many grams of a **solute** can be dissolved in 100 grams of **solvent**.

The effect of temperature

The solubility of a substance is different at different temperatures. Most substances are more soluble in hot solvents than in cold solvents.

More sugar will dissolve in hot coffee than in cold coffee.

Stirring

Why do people stir sugar when they add it to coffee? Stirring does not make more sugar dissolve, but it does speed up the dissolving process!

Stirring does not increase the solubility of a substance. The same amount of solute will eventually dissolve whether it is stirred or not, but if you don't stir, it will take much longer!

Saturated solutions

If you add a spoonful of salt to water, it will dissolve. If you keep adding more and more salt, without adding any more water, you will eventually get to a point where no more salt will dissolve. All the spaces between the water **molecules** are full. This is called a **saturated** solution.

The **particles** of salt that don't dissolve will swirl around while you are stirring, but eventually they will settle out and form a layer of salt on the bottom of the container.

Try This!

Growing crystals

Try this to grow crystals from a saturated solution.

You will need a jar, hot water, table salt, a pencil, and string.

1. Put very hot water (be careful!) into a jar so it is two-thirds full.

2. Add table salt and keep adding until no more will dissolve.

3. Cut a piece of string and tie a loop in one end.

4. Tie the other end of the string around a pencil.

5. Balance the pencil on the rim

of the jar so that your loop is well covered by the salt solution.

6. Leave it for a few days in a place where it will not be disturbed.

7. Lift your string out of the solution— it should be covered in crystals.

Try it again, but add food coloring to the solution to get colored crystals!

SEPARATING MIXTURES

Because the substances in a mixture are not joined together, they can be separated from each other. There are several different methods for doing this. The method used depends on the properties of the mixture and the substances that it contains.

Sedimentation

How would you separate a mixture of sand and water? This could be separated by **sedimentation**. The mixture is left undisturbed in a container. The sand slowly settles on the bottom of the container. The water can then be poured off carefully, leaving the sand behind.

At water treatment plants, dirty water is cleaned until it is ready to be used again. Part of this process is sedimentation. The dirty water is left to stand in large tanks. **Debris** (loose material) falls to the bottom of the tank and is removed. The water can be drained off, ready for the next cleaning stage.

Dirt and debris will sink in this settling tank, leaving cleaner water at the top.

Filtration

How would you separate a mixture of coffee grounds and water? This could be separated by **filtration**. The mixture is poured into a funnel that is lined with a material such as paper. The **liquid** drains through the paper and the **solid** is left behind. The liquid that is collected is called the **filtrate**. The solid that is left behind is called the **residue**.

Coffee filters use filtration. Hot water and ground coffee beans are mixed together. Small **particles** of coffee mix with the water and make a mixture of liquid coffee. The liquid coffee drains through the filter into the container below. This is the filtrate. The rest of the coffee grounds are left behind in the paper. They are the residue.

The solid coffee grounds are held back by the paper filter. The liquid coffee passes through and collects in the glass carafe.

Evaporation

How could you separate salt from seawater? **Evaporation** can be used to separate the substances in a **solution** like this.

How does evaporation work?

Evaporation is a process in which a liquid substance changes state to become a **gas**. If you leave a liquid in an open container, some of its particles at the surface will change to gas and escape into the air. If you leave it long enough, all the liquid will disappear into the air. Anything that was **dissolved** in the liquid will be left behind.

Speeding up evaporation

Heating a liquid makes it evaporate more quickly. You can see this happening if you heat a saucepan of water: steam rises from the surface of the water as it gets hot.

Using evaporation

Some of the salt in your food has probably been collected by evaporation! Around the world, companies leave saltwater to stand in lakes. The water evaporates, leaving solid salt behind. This is then cleaned and purified before being sold.

These piles of salt have been collected from saltwater by evaporation.

Try This!

Getting salt back!

Try this to get salt back from a salt solution.

You will need a cup, warm water, salt, a spoon, and a saucer.

1 Pour some warm water into a cup.

2 Add a few spoonfuls of salt and stir until it has dissolved.

3 Pour some of your salt solution onto a saucer.

4 Put the saucer in a warm (but not enclosed) place—a sunny windowsill or a shelf above a warm radiator would be ideal.

5 Check the saucer each day. You should see that the water level falls. This is because the water is evaporating into the air.

6 After several days, you should start to see salt crystals appearing.

7 After a few more days, the saucer will be completely dry. All the water has evaporated, and you have got back the salt you started with!

Distillation

Distillation is a way of separating and collecting a **solvent** from a solution. The solution is heated until the solvent evaporates, leaving the **solute** behind. The evaporated solvent is then **condensed** and collected.

How does distillation work?

The solution is put in a closed container with a pipe leading out just below the top. The solution is heated, and the solvent evaporates and becomes a gas. Anything that was dissolved in it is left behind. The gas rises to the top of the container but cannot escape. Some moves out into the pipe. This leads into a tube called a **condenser**. This is a tube where the temperature is cooled by a **coolant**, such as water. This makes the gas turn back into liquid. It drips into a container and is collected.

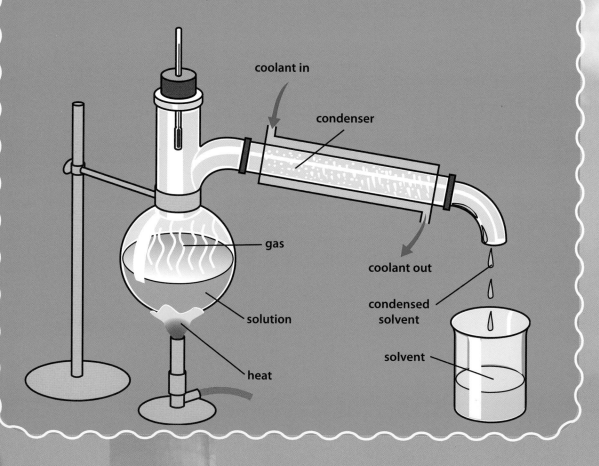

coolant in

condenser

gas

coolant out

solution

condensed solvent

heat

solvent

Try This!

Turn dirty water into clean water!

This activity uses sedimentation, filtration, and distillation.

You will need:
- 3 clean jars, one with a tight-fitting lid
- about a cup of garden soil or earth
- small plastic container
- a sieve
- paper towels
- plastic film

1. **Sedimentation:** Shake together half a jar of water and the soil. Leave the jar to stand for a few hours, until the biggest materials have settled at the bottom of the jar. Carefully pour the liquid into a clean jar.

2. **Filtration:** Line a sieve with several layers of kitchen towel. Set it over another jar. Pour the liquid into the sieve. The liquid will go through, leaving small pieces of dirt on the towel.

3. **Distillation:** Cover the top of the jar with plastic film. The film should be stretched tightly across the top of the jar. Leave the jar in a warm place and look at it again in a few hours.

Drops of water should have collected on the underside of the plastic film.

This is water that evaporated from the solution then cooled and turned back into liquid water.

WARNING

Do not drink your "clean" water. It may not be clean enough to drink!

Getting Clean Water

What do you do if you are surrounded by salty seawater but have no fresh water to drink? Easy! You get rid of the salt and get water that is pure enough to drink. This process is called desalination.

From seawater to tap water

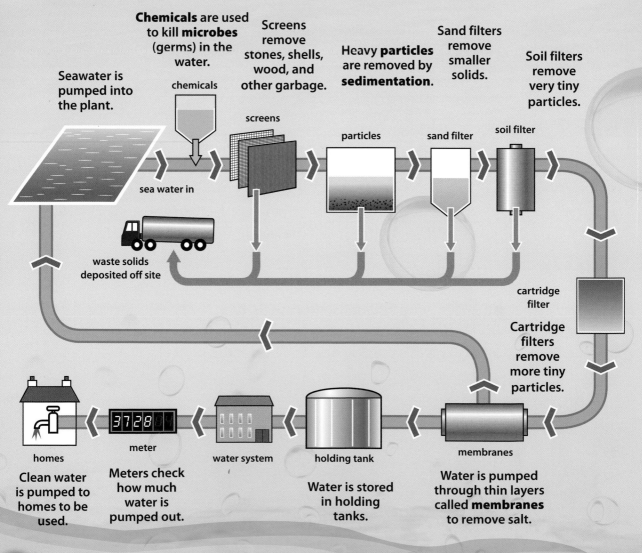

Seawater is pumped into the plant.

Chemicals are used to kill **microbes** (germs) in the water.

Screens remove stones, shells, wood, and other garbage.

Heavy **particles** are removed by **sedimentation**.

Sand filters remove smaller solids.

Soil filters remove very tiny particles.

chemicals

sea water in

screens

particles

sand filter

soil filter

waste solids deposited off site

cartridge filter

Cartridge filters remove more tiny particles.

homes

Clean water is pumped to homes to be used.

meter

3728 04

Meters check how much water is pumped out.

water system

holding tank

Water is stored in holding tanks.

membranes

Water is pumped through thin layers called **membranes** to remove salt.

AMAZING FACTS!

● There are more than 13,000 desalination plants around the world. Together, they produce more than 54 billion liters (14 billion gallons) of water every day. This helps people who live in places where there is not enough water. But many people think desalination is not a good thing because it is expensive, uses a lot of energy, and may harm the environment.

● Desalination plants use a lot of energy—but some small ones are now solar powered. This means that they are run by power from the Sun. Some other plants are powered using biofuels. This is a type of fuel made using natural products.

● Many large ships have desalination plants on board. They provide a constant supply of fresh water from seawater. This means the ship has enough water for its crew and passengers and does not need to have large water tanks on board.

This desalination plant takes the salt out of seawater to provide a supply of clean drinking water.

OIL DISTILLATION

Oil is a mixture of many different substances. Before these substances can be used, they must be separated. This is done by a process called fractional distillation.

How does fractional distillation work?

Fractional distillation is the process of separating a **chemical compound** into its different parts, or fractions. Look at the diagram opposite. The stages are numbered and explained below.

1 Crude oil is heated to 600°C (1,112°F) in a furnace. The oil boils and most of the substances it contains turn to **gases**.

2 Gases from the boiling oil enter the bottom of a fractional distillation column. The column is hot at the bottom and cool at the top.

3 The gases cool as they rise. When each gas reaches the height in the column that matches its own boiling point, it **condenses**, or turns back into a **liquid**.

4 At each level, the different liquids are collected and piped out of the column. Each collected liquid is called a fraction.

BOILING POINTS

Every substance has its own boiling point. This is the temperature at which it changes from a liquid into a gas. When a gas is cooling down, this is also the point at which it condenses, or changes back into a liquid.

Fractional distillation of oil

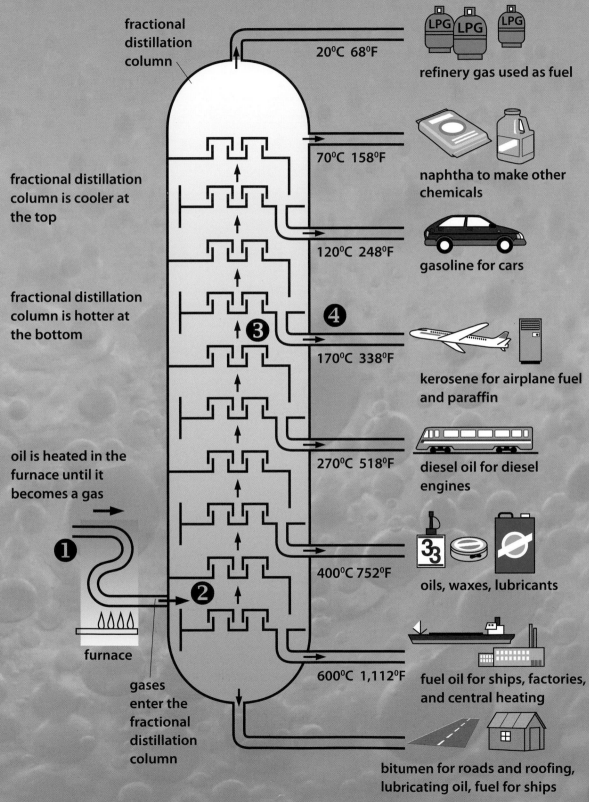

fractional distillation column

20°C 68°F

refinery gas used as fuel

70°C 158°F

naphtha to make other chemicals

fractional distillation column is cooler at the top

120°C 248°F

gasoline for cars

fractional distillation column is hotter at the bottom

170°C 338°F

kerosene for airplane fuel and paraffin

oil is heated in the furnace until it becomes a gas

270°C 518°F

diesel oil for diesel engines

400°C 752°F

oils, waxes, lubricants

furnace

600°C 1,112°F

fuel oil for ships, factories, and central heating

gases enter the fractional distillation column

bitumen for roads and roofing, lubricating oil, fuel for ships

Chromatography

Chromatography is another method that can be used to separate the different chemicals in a solution. It works because some chemicals in the solution are more attracted to the solvent than others. The more a chemical is attracted to the solvent, the farther it will travel up the support.

Try This!

What's in your pens?

Try this to find out which colored inks your felt pens contain.

You will need several wide-rimmed jars or pots, blotting paper or a paper towel, pencils, nonwaterproof felt pens, scissors, and sticky tape.

 1 Cut a strip of your paper. It should be just long enough to touch the bottom of the jar.

2 Use a felt pen to draw a line across the strip about two centimeters (one inch) up from the bottom.

 3 Fasten the top of the strip around a pencil with tape.

4 Fill the jar with about a centimeter (half an inch) of water. Rest the pencil on the top of the jar so the pen line is just above the water level.

5 Leave the strip in the water until the water has nearly reached the top of it.

6 Lift the pencil up to take the strip out of the water. Hang it up to dry.

The water moves up the paper, through the pen line. Some chemicals in the ink are more attracted to the water than others. They travel farther than others. The different chemicals in the ink will separate into bands. You have separated the ink into the different colored chemicals that it contains!

This is the result of a chromatography test done with lots of different inks.

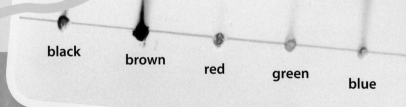

black   brown   red   green   blue

Next, you could try this with food colorings or fruit juices.

Different chromatography methods

Not all **mixtures** can be separated using water and paper. Instead, chromatography can be carried out using other materials.

Some chemicals do not **dissolve** in water, so water cannot be used to separate them. Other solvents must be used instead. For example, acetone, alcohol, vinegar, and turpentine all can be used instead of water.

Some chemicals travel more easily through gel, so this can be used instead of paper.

Using chromatography

Chromatography is used to separate many different mixtures, including:

- water samples, to check for pollution and find out whether they contain any dangerous chemicals

- dyes, to see exactly which colors they contain

- blood or urine, to see whether a person's blood or urine contains **banned** drugs

- medicines, to check that they do not contain any unwanted chemicals

- foods, to check that they do not contain anything harmful

These scientists are using chromatography equipment to separate mixtures of chemicals.

TAKE CARE!

When samples are tested, the scientists need to be very sure that their results are accurate. The sample must be collected, transported, and tested without getting mixed with anything else.

To check for accuracy, scientists often test samples called "controls." They know what is in the control samples, and so they know what their results should show. If their results are different, it means they have done something wrong!

Each drop of liquid is counted to make sure every sample is exactly the same.

CHROMATOGRAPHY AND CRIMES

Chromatography can help detectives solve crimes! Here's just one way in which it is useful . . .

Drugs or not?

Suppose a detective has found a packet of powder at a crime scene. Does it contain illegal drugs? The detective sends it to the **forensic laboratory** for testing. The investigation might follow this process:

1. The powder is mixed with a **solvent** to **dissolve** it.

2. The **solution** is filtered to remove any undissolved **chemicals**.

3. The filtered solution is heated and pushed through a **gas** chromatography tube.

4. Some chemicals travel through the column more quickly than others.

5. When each chemical reaches the end of the tube, it passes into a scanning machine.

6. The scanning machine shows the pattern of each chemical on a screen.

7. The forensic scientists compare the patterns with those of known drugs.

8. If the pattern matches that of a particular drug, the scientists know that the crime scene sample contained that drug.

Forensic scientists use chromatography to identify drugs.

Drug testing

Many drugs are banned in athletic competitions. Athletes are tested regularly to make sure they are not breaking the rules. They give a blood, urine, or hair sample. The most common test is on urine. The urine sample is heated until it changes into a gas. This is pushed through a tube filled with **silica** (a hard **unreactive compound** that occurs naturally). Some chemicals pass through the tube more quickly than others. The separated chemicals then enter a scanner. Each chemical has its own special scanning pattern. If a drug is present in the sample, it will be detected by its scanning pattern.

Chromatography is used to analyze samples from athletes when testing for banned drugs.

DISCOVERY TIMELINE

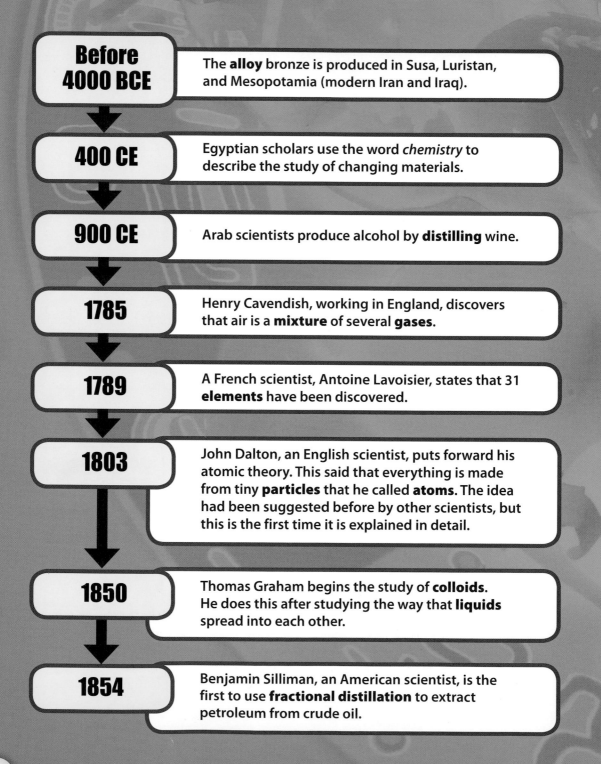

Before 4000 BCE

The **alloy** bronze is produced in Susa, Luristan, and Mesopotamia (modern Iran and Iraq).

400 CE

Egyptian scholars use the word *chemistry* to describe the study of changing materials.

900 CE

Arab scientists produce alcohol by **distilling** wine.

1785

Henry Cavendish, working in England, discovers that air is a **mixture** of several **gases**.

1789

A French scientist, Antoine Lavoisier, states that 31 **elements** have been discovered.

1803

John Dalton, an English scientist, puts forward his atomic theory. This said that everything is made from tiny **particles** that he called **atoms**. The idea had been suggested before by other scientists, but this is the first time it is explained in detail.

1850

Thomas Graham begins the study of **colloids**. He does this after studying the way that **liquids** spread into each other.

1854

Benjamin Silliman, an American scientist, is the first to use **fractional distillation** to extract petroleum from crude oil.

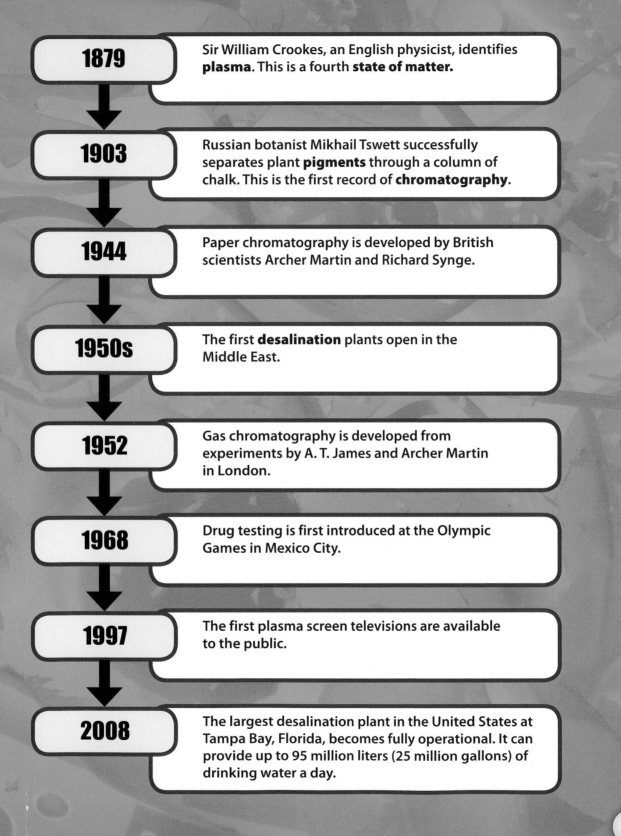

1879	Sir William Crookes, an English physicist, identifies **plasma**. This is a fourth **state of matter.**
1903	Russian botanist Mikhail Tswett successfully separates plant **pigments** through a column of chalk. This is the first record of **chromatography**.
1944	Paper chromatography is developed by British scientists Archer Martin and Richard Synge.
1950s	The first **desalination** plants open in the Middle East.
1952	Gas chromatography is developed from experiments by A. T. James and Archer Martin in London.
1968	Drug testing is first introduced at the Olympic Games in Mexico City.
1997	The first plasma screen televisions are available to the public.
2008	The largest desalination plant in the United States at Tampa Bay, Florida, becomes fully operational. It can provide up to 95 million liters (25 million gallons) of drinking water a day.

Summary

Here is a summary of what you have learned about mixtures and solutions!

What is a mixture?

Mixtures contain two or more things mixed together. They can be **solids, liquids**, or **gases**. The **particles** of the substances in a mixture are not joined to each other.

Homogeneous mixtures are the same throughout. **Heterogeneous** mixtures are not the same throughout.

Solutions

A solution is a homogeneous mixture. When one substance is mixed into another to form a solution, we say it **dissolves**.

The substance that dissolves is the **solute**. The substance in which it dissolves is the **solvent**.

Nothing is lost or gained when a substance dissolves. The mass of the solution is the same as the mass of the solute + the mass of the solvent.

Some substances dissolve in one solvent but not in others.

Solubility

Solubility is a measure of how much solute will dissolve in a solvent.

Most substances are more soluble in hot solvents than in cold solvents.

Stirring does NOT increase the solubility of a substance—it just helps to speed up the dissolving process.

A **saturated** solution is made when no more substance will dissolve in a solvent.

Separating mixtures

Sedimentation: if a mixture of a solid in a liquid is left to stand, the solid will eventually settle at the bottom. The liquid can be poured off.

Filtration: if a mixture of a solid in a liquid is poured through a filter, the liquid passes through the filter but the solid is trapped in the filter.

Evaporation: if a solution is left to stand, liquid particles escape into the air, leaving behind anything that was dissolved in the liquid.

Distillation: if a solution is heated, the solvent will evaporate leaving the solute behind. The solvent is cooled and collected.

Chromatography

Paper **chromatography** can be used to separate mixtures of liquids, such as colored inks. As the solvent moves up the paper, it carries some substances farther than others.

Glossary

aerosol suspension of liquid droplets or fine solid particles in a gas

alloy solid solution made by melting and mixing a metal and one or more additional elements

atom tiny particle of a substance. Atoms can join together to make larger particles called molecules.

banned forbidden

biofuel fuel made from living matter, such as plants

chemical substance with a certain chemical composition

chemical reaction change that produces a new substance

chromatography method of separating mixtures

colloid a mixture in which the particles are not dissolved, but do not settle out

compound substance made from atoms of two or more elements

condense to turn from a gas into a liquid

condenser part of a distillation set-up that condenses a vapor

coolant liquid that is used to decrease temperature

debris scattered remains of something

desalination removal of salt from salt water to obtain fresh water

dissolve to mix two substances together so that the particles of one spread out between the particles of the other

distillation collection of solvent after evaporation

element substance made from a single type of atom

evaporation escape of particles of a liquid into the air

filtrate liquid that is collected during filtration

filtration separation of a mixture by passing it through a filter

forensic laboratory room where scientific experiments take place that might provide evidence for criminal investigations

fractional distillation process of separating a compound into its different parts, or fractions

gas state of matter in which the substance can flow, change shape, and be squashed

heterogeneous not the same throughout

homogeneous same throughout

human-made something that is produced by people and does not occur naturally

immiscible describes substances that cannot be mixed together

insoluble will not dissolve

liquid state of matter in which the substance can flow and change shape but cannot be squashed

membrane very thin layer

metal substance that is usually hard and shiny, and will conduct heat and electricity

microbes tiny organisms that can cause disease

mixture two or more substances mixed together

molecule particle made from two or more atoms joined together

particle tiny part of a substance

pigment substance that gives something its color

plasma state of matter in which gas atoms start to break down

property characteristic of something

residue solid that is collected during filtration

saturated when a solution is so full of a solute that no more can be dissolved in it

sedimentation settling out of a solid from a mixture

silica hard, colorless compound that is found naturally

solid state of matter in which the substance cannot flow, change shape, or be squashed

solubility amount of a substance that will dissolve in a solvent

soluble able to dissolve in a solvent

solute solid that dissolves to form a solution

solution liquid that has something dissolved in it

solvent liquid in which a solid dissolves to form a solution

state of matter form of a substance as a solid, liquid, gas, or plasma

support substance used to separate chemicals in chromatography

suspension mixture in which particles of one substance are spread throughout another substance but do not dissolve and will eventually settle out

unreactive unlikely to react chemically

Find Out More

Topics to research

Why not try to find out more about some of the topics in this book? Here are some questions to help you get started.

- Desalination plants are used all over the world. Where are the biggest desalination plants? How many homes and businesses do they supply with clean water? This website might help you find out:
  http://www.water-technology.net/projects/durrat-desalination/

- There are many types of alloys. What are "smart" alloys? This website will help you find out more about them:
  http://www.gcsescience.com/ex37.htm

- When a tanker carrying oil gets into trouble in the sea, it might spill oil into the sea. Sea creatures, such as seabirds or seals, get covered with the oil and have trouble swimming and feeding. People try and help the sea creatures by cleaning the oil off them. How can oil be cleaned off seabirds? This website will help you find out more about oil spills:
  http://www.ec.gc.ca/envirozine/english/issues/50/feature2_e.cfm

- Plasma, the fourth state of matter, can be used in many ways. How is plasma used around you everyday? This website will help you find out more about plasma:
  http://www.chem4kids.com/files/matter_plasma.html

- Acid rain affects countries all over the world. How are different places affected by acid rain? What can be done to try and prevent it? This website will help you find out more about acid rain:
  http://www.ypte.org.uk/environmental/acid-rain/1

Books to read

Aloian, Molly. *Why Chemistry Matters: Mixtures and Solutions,*
    NY: Crabtree Publishing Co. 2008.

Baldwin, Carol. *Material Matters (Raintree Freestyle): Compounds, Mixtures, and Solutions,*
    Chicago: Raintree Publishers, 2005.

Karpelenia, Jenny. *Reading Essentials in Science: Mixtures and Solutions,* Logan, IA: Perfection
    Learning, 2005.

Rodgers, K. *Internet-Linked Library of Science: Mixtures and Compounds,*
    Usborne Publishing Ltd, 2001.

Spilsbury, Louise and Richard Spilsbury. *Building Blocks of Matter: Mixtures and Solutions,*
    Chicago: Heinemann, 2007.

Websites

http://www.chem4kids.com/
Website for young people, with information and quizzes about all aspects of chemistry.

http://www.bbc.co.uk/schools/ks3bitesize/science/chemistry/elements_com_mix_6.shtml
Website with information, diagrams, animations, games, and quizzes about mixtures,
solutions, and other chemistry topics.

http://www.docbrown.info/page01/ElCpdMix/EleCmdMix.htm
Website with detailed information, revision notes, and quizzes about many different science
topics including mixtures and solutions.

Index